Original title:
The Brightness Between Us

Copyright © 2025 Creative Arts Management OÜ
All rights reserved.

Author: Sebastian Whitmore
ISBN HARDBACK: 978-3-69081-151-4
ISBN PAPERBACK: 978-3-69081-647-2

Radiant Spaces Between Us

In the gap where laughter hides,
We toss our jokes like frisbees wide.
A punchline here, a giggle there,
We float on quirks, without a care.

In a dance of thoughts so bright,
We fumble words, yet it feels right.
With silly faces and silly rhymes,
We share our hearts, in joyful times.

Glimmers of Shared Dreams

In dreams where we both play the fool,
We race on clouds, our own cool tool.
A rainbow slide that never ends,
With candy thoughts, the world we blend.

Our hopes are balloons that float so high,
In balloon fights, we touch the sky.
With giggles echoing through the night,
Our dreams become the purest light.

Sweet Illuminations of Trust

In this trust, we stumble, we grunt,
Finding joy in every hunt.
With secrets tucked in silly socks,
In our own world, we're paradox rocks.

Through whispered tales beneath the stars,
We share our quirks, our battle scars.
With every laugh, we stitch a seam,
In every shared mishap, we gleam.

The Warmth of Connected Souls

In this warmth, we roast our fears,
With marshmallow tales and jelly cheers.
Around the fire, we tell our tales,
Of pizza mishaps and silly fails.

With every grin and every pun,
We chase the night 'til morning sun.
In this glow, we twirl and sway,
Connected in the funniest way.

Timeless Rays of Connection

In the sunbeam of your smile,
I find my socks that went astray.
They dance like ninjas on the floor,
While we both laugh and play.

Your laughter sparkles like confetti,
It flies around like dizzy bees.
I tripped over my own two feet,
You giggled, "That's just how it is!"

We paint our world with silly hats,
Your cat wears mine, quite a sight!
We waltz like stars in this silly tale,
Making mundane moments bright.

Even time can't help but grin,
As we chase the jolly glow.
In this timeless circus we create,
Our connection steals the show!

Resonance of Luminosity

When you trip and make a scene,
I laugh so hard, I hit the ground.
Your clumsiness is quite a skill,
Like a new dance we just found!

You wear that hat with vibrant flair,
A polka-dotted majestic crown.
While I question who wore it first,
You just claim it, with no frown.

In the glow of twilight's quilt,
We chase fireflies with wild delight.
Your shouts echo in the night sky,
Turning mischief into light.

The universe can't damp our glee,
As we trip through the cosmic fun.
Each moment shines, a spark divine,
With you, my friend, my favorite sun!

Serendipity's Illuminated Path

We tripped over laughter, what a sweet fall,
Like socks that don't match at a formal ball.
A random collision, a slip, then a grin,
You spilled all your secrets, I let mine begin.

Each twist that we take, we giggle and sway,
Chasing our shadows, in a silly ballet.
Your hat's on my head, and I'm slipping on shoes,
Together we wander, sipping wild views.

Moonlit Conversations

Under the stars, we hatched a grand scheme,
To convince the moon that we'd make a great team.
You said with a wink, it needs proper flare,
So we tossed up confetti, threw joy in the air.

Your jokes like comets, they zipped and they zipped,
While I clutched my sides, nearly lost in the script.
A waltz with the crickets, we danced in delight,
Our giggles the music, way past midnight.

A Kaleidoscope of Moments

Life's a wild painting, with splatters and swirls,
Like mismatched socks on a parade of girls.
Each twist is a color, each turn a new hue,
We burst into fits over coffee and stew.

The canvas of friendship, so bright and so bold,
With memories splashed, a treasure to hold.
You made punchlines dance under coffee shop lights,
And I just kept laughing, till we spotted the kites.

Glowing in Each Other's Eyes

In the flicker of dawn, with sleepy surprise,
We found all the giggles that glow in our eyes.
You stole my toast, said it needed a friend,
I promised to share, but I scrapped that in the end.

With pancakes like planets, and syrupy moons,
We cooked up our shenanigans, humming old tunes.
Each bite filled with sparkle, each laugh shared just right,
Who knew mornings could shine with such silly delight?

Sunbeams of Unison

In a world where socks unite,
Worn on feet, what a sight!
We dance like lightning bugs,
Buzzing laughter, all snug.

Our giggles rise like dough,
While we steal the show.
Chasing rainbows on a whim,
With a playful little grin.

Together we span like ribbons,
Twisting with light, not a given.
Each joke a star in the night,
Lighting up all that's bright.

With pies flying through the air,
We revel without a care.
In this whimsical parade,
Friendship's light is made.

Harmonious Reflections

In mirrors cracked, reflections gleam,
Like pop flies in a baseball dream.
We juggle quirks and silly bets,
A symphony of laughs, no regrets.

Sunshine spills in every crack,
Chasing shadows, never lack.
Our voices blend like peanut butter,
With each quip, the laughter's a flutter.

With every joke thrown like darts,
Sprinkling joy in all the parts.
We echo giggles, give and take,
In this rhythm, smiles awake.

Our playlist? Funny faces and puns,
Creating light as bright as the suns.
In this dance of silly cheer,
We find magic, crystal clear.

Luminescent Journeys Together

On a road paved by our giggles,
Where every bump is a wiggle.
We ride bicycles made of dreams,
Sailing through ice cream streams.

Each turn brings a funny sight,
Vertigo from delight!
With jellybeans guiding our quest,
Sprinting forward, never rest.

Catching sun through rainbow glasses,
While the world just subtly passes.
Our laughter echoes, a beacon bright,
In this adventure, all feels right.

We collect moments like fireflies,
Glowing memories, oh so high.
In every twist, we sprinkle glee,
That's the real magic, can't you see?

A Mosaic of Light

From scattered bits of fun and mirth,
We build a world with plenty of girth.
Each chuckle fits like a puzzle piece,
Crafting joy that will never cease.

In this canvas where colors blend,
We create things that never end.
With laughter's brush, we splash it wide,
A masterpiece with cheer inside.

As rainbows stretch across the sky,
Our playful spirits learn to fly.
With each pun we ought to share,
We weave a quilt of love and care.

Hand in hand, we skip a beat,
Life's funny tunes keep us on our feet.
In this warmth, we shine so bright,
Creating magic, pure delight.

Memories Like Fireflies

In jars we caught our laughter,
And released it into the night.
Each giggle shone like a beacon,
Dancing in soft moonlight.

We trip over our own shadows,
Chasing whispers of delight.
With fireflies and silly faces,
We twinkle, oh what a sight!

Our stories flicker like lanterns,
As we recount our clumsy falls.
In the magic of our moments,
Even the smallest spark enthralls.

So let's bottle-up our silly,
And toast to everything we've done.
With mischief as our guide,
We'll always find the fun.

Love's Luminous Journey

We travel roads of glitter,
With sparkles at our feet.
Each step fills the world with laughter,
Every bump an amusing feat.

Our love's a glowing circus,
With clowns that trip and fall.
We juggle silly moments,
Together through it all.

In the tent of crazy dreams,
We dance like no one sees.
With each chuckle that escapes,
Our hearts are sure to tease.

So here's to our bright journey,
With sunshine in our eyes.
We'll skip through life like children,
With laughter as our prize.

Lightly Woven Dreams

In a quilt of quirky wishes,
We stitch the night with glee.
Each thread a silly memory,
Woven just for you and me.

We twirl in patches of laughter,
In this fabric so divine.
With every snip and every stitch,
Our joy becomes the line.

Underneath a glowing moon,
We giggle at our schemes.
In a tapestry of wild fun,
We drape our stitched-up dreams.

So let's wrap up our adventures,
In a blanket full of cheer.
With zany stitches binding us,
Together, year by year.

Unseen Threads of Connection

Invisible strings between us,
Tug gently at our hearts.
They weave through all our laughter,
Creating perfect arts.

In a world of crazy mishaps,
We dance like no one's there.
With every twist and tumble,
We fill the air with flair.

Our bond is like a yo-yo,
Bouncing back with every jest.
We're tethered by our humor,
Together, we're the best.

So here's to unseen magic,
In our silly little spree.
We'll spin through life with giggles,
In joyful harmony.

Heartbeats in the Glow

In the dark, we dance and sway,
Laughter bouncing in the fray.
Like two stars in silly flight,
Bouncing quirks, oh what a sight!

Every joke, a shining spark,
Turning silence into lark.
When we're close, the world can't see,
Just how goofy we can be!

Our heartbeat quickens, not in fear,
But at a joke that's drawing near.
In the glow, we find our pace,
Making funny faces with grace!

As we stumble, trip, and cheer,
The love between us grows sincere.
In this glow, we're never shy,
With every giggle, we just fly!

Rays of Mutual Understanding

Underneath the sunlight's gleam,
We plot and scheme a goofy dream.
With a wink and cheeky grin,
We know where the fun begins!

We share our snacks, you take the fries,
And I'll claim the cookies, no surprise.
With a laugh, we trade it fair,
Companions in this feeding dare!

In our world, it's all a game,
Where we both share the same old name.
With our quirks, we light the day,
In a marvelous, silly way!

So here's to rays of joy we make,
In every giggle and funny shake.
Together we spark the brightest cheer,
With each madcap moment, we draw near!

Firelight of Friendship

Around the fire, tales unfold,
Of trips and trips, both brave and bold.
With marshmallows, we poke and pry,
Silly stories, oh my my!

S'mores are melting, laughter roars,
As we stumble out of doors.
In the flicker, shadows play,
As our silliness leads the way!

In the warmth, we find our place,
With every grin, a soft embrace.
Through the sparks, our laughter flies,
Soon, napkin fights, oh what a prize!

With every joke, we mend the night,
In the glow, all feels so right.
In this firelight, we're alive,
Twinkling like stars, we will survive!

Celestial Conversations

Under stars, we share our dreams,
With giggles echoing in moonbeams.
Discussion turns to playful jest,
In this universe, we're blessed!

You say Pluto's not a planet?
We argue it's just been slanted!
With every point, we crack a smile,
In our galaxy, we'll stay awhile!

As constellations start to twirl,
Our dialogue begins to swirl.
In this cosmic, silly fight,
We find joy in endless night!

So here's to stars that shine so bright,
In conversations full of light.
With each comet that zooms by,
We make wishes, and oh my!

Glowing Dimensions of Us

In the space between your jokes,
I find the light that truly pokes.
Laughter dances in the air,
Like fireflies without a care.

A bright balloon we both have tied,
It floats around and waves with pride.
Chasing shadows, we both race,
With silly grins upon our face.

The sun bows down to giggles free,
As we weave tales of you and me.
Our quirks like stars in evening skies,
Illuminate this bond that flies.

Each shared glance, a spark so bright,
Turns the mundane into delight.
With every crack and every smile,
We light up the world, mile by mile.

Heartstrings in Radiance

Your puns align like constellations,
Creating joy through wild sensations.
With every quirk and silly tease,
We play our tune with perfect ease.

When you trip over nothing at all,
I laugh so hard, I almost fall.
Yet, in this mess of laughter's glow,
Our heartstrings hum, oh, how they flow.

We dance on clouds made out of dreams,
Where nothing is ever as it seems.
With every twirl, your smile's the tune,
Under the watchful gaze of the moon.

So let's concoct our funny sketches,
Stand out like stars in velvet sketches.
Together, we light the silly way,
In colors bright, come what may.

Aurora of Unspoken Words

In a world where silence sings,
Your laughter flies on cheeky wings.
Words unspoken do jump and twirl,
Like swirling colors in a whirl.

We grin like kids on merry-go-rounds,
Finding joy in the silliest sounds.
Every glance a playful tease,
With radiant sparks that always please.

From gentle jokes to playful smirks,
Our unique rhythm truly works.
An aurora lights the shadows deep,
Awakening smiles as we leap.

So here we stand, bright and bold,
Sharing moments that never get old.
In this amusing cosmic dance,
Our unspoken bond takes a chance.

Harmonies Under Starlight

Under starlight, we play the fools,
Breaking all of the so-called rules.
Each giggle lights up the night,
Transforming shadows into sight.

With every pun and playful jive,
Like fireflies, we feel alive.
The moon winks at our joyful dance,
In this symphony of chance.

Twinkle, twinkle, little laugh,
You're the perfect, silly half.
As we rhyme through cosmic waves,
This laughter's light forever saves.

So hold my hand, let's take a trip,
On cloud nine, we laugh and skip.
Together, we create the tune,
Of harmony in the bright moon.

Radiance of Connection

In a world where socks vanish,
And mismatched pairs reign supreme,
Our laughs light up the darkness,
Like a disco ball's wild gleam.

You send me a meme at midnight,
I respond with a dad joke,
Together we weave a tapestry,
Of silliness and pure smoke.

Friendship shines like pizza grease,
Greasy but oh so divine,
We may be weird, and that's okay,
Your quirks are just like mine!

Through awkward moments and blunders,
We twirl like balloons in the sky,
With you, life's a merry circus,
Where laughter will never die.

Luminous Threads

Threads of stories zig and zag,
Like noodles in a soup,
Your laughter's a catchy tune,
As we dance in a noodle loop.

We share secrets wrapped in giggles,
Like candy in a bright bowl,
Each glance is a spark of joy,
Tickling the depths of our soul.

The quirks you possess are treasures,
Like finding cash in a coat,
With your absurd tales of cats,
You keep my spirits afloat.

In this chaotic game of life,
We twine like spaghetti strands,
The luminous threads of friendship,
Hold together our goofy plans.

Celestial Echoes

Bouncing jokes like shooting stars,
Across the night sky so wide,
Your puns are comets of gold,
Making giggle-bellies glide.

In the galaxy of mischief,
We orbit around the same sun,
Making memes that are out of this world,
Contagious joy, oh what fun!

With every chat, we light up space,
Like aliens at a disco ball,
Your laughter is the cosmic dust,
Creating a universe for us all.

Together we're a pair of moons,
Spinning 'round in a quirky dance,
Our friendship's a stellar echo,
In this vast, whacky expanse.

Glimmers of Affection

Hints of hilarity sparkle,
Like glitter on a birthday cake,
With you, every moment's a laugh,
Even mistakes we happily make.

We share a bond like jellybeans,
Sweet and a bit too much,
In the kitchen of our friendship,
Every word is a perfect touch.

Dancing in the rain of errors,
With umbrellas made of dreams,
Each giggle is a drop of joy,
Fueling our whimsical schemes.

So let's take the stage together,
In our comedy club of two,
Glimmers of affection shine bright,
In all the silly things we do.

Soulshine Symphony

In a world of mismatched socks,
We dance like two silly clocks.
With laughter that fills the air,
You shine, oh friend, beyond compare.

Our jokes like fireworks ignite,
In the chaos, we find pure delight.
You trip, I laugh, the moment's grand,
Together, a duet so well planned.

Each quirk is a note in our tune,
Barking dogs sing under the moon.
With puns that could make a crow caw,
Our friendship's the best comedy, ha-ha!

Lemonade spills on the floor,
As we dance like it's a wild chore.
With sprinkles of joy in our hair,
Life's a feast, and we're the fair!

Where Hearts Converge

In a café, where we sip and smile,
Your antics can stretch a mile.
You spill your drink, it lands on me,
We laugh until we can't see.

We trade our snacks, a sweet exchange,
Your taste, dear friend, is just so strange.
But every bite brings shared delight,
In this giggle-filled, cozy night.

You wear that hat, oh what a sight,
In your world, everything feels right.
With playful jests and silly tales,
Our laughter blows like gentle gales.

With doodles on napkins, our art's a mess,
Yet every squiggle, I must confess,
Is a treasure, a laughter escape,
Drawing smiles, no need for tape!

A Spectrum of Touch

A tickle fight breaks out in spring,
You laugh, I yell, it's a joyful thing.
With playful pokes beneath the sun,
We banter 'til the day is done.

Your hug is like a cozy blanket,
And when you dance, it's not a prank yet.
With every nudge, our spirits soar,
Bound by laughter, oh let's do more!

Our high-fives could break down walls,
In this silly game, nobody falls.
From cheeky winks to funny grins,
A touch of joy, where laughter begins.

Hold my hand as we spin around,
In this whirl of giggles, joy is found.
Together we're a colorful sketch,
In this bond, who needs a fetch?

Stars in Our Eyes

With twinkling eyes like constellations,
We share dreams and silly creations.
You draw a mustache on the moon,
And we burst forth in laughter's tune.

In the galaxy of our delight,
Running through the fields at night.
Tripping over roots, giggles ensue,
You say, 'They're just looking for a cue!'

Our wishes tossed into the night,
Magical moments feel so right.
You sing off-key, but who really cares?
We're stars together; it's laughter we share.

Chasing fireflies, catching the glow,
With every step, our spirits grow.
You say, 'Life's a stage with no disguise,'
Our friendship shines, like stars in our eyes!

Threads of Golden Affection

In a world where socks do hide,
I found your heart, tucked inside.
A mismatched pair, but still they glow,
With laughter shared, our love will grow.

Like spaghetti flung on kitchen walls,
Our silly antics break down the stalls.
You dance like jelly, I trip on air,
Yet in your gaze, I find my flair.

We juggle flames, yet never burn,
With every joke, there's more to learn.
Our shenanigans light up the room,
Together we bloom, like flowers in bloom.

In the chaos, a bond so tight,
With every quirk, we take to flight.
Like peanut butter and jelly art,
You and I, we're a funny part.

Nocturnal Rays of Togetherness

Under moon's gaze, we plot our pranks,
While the stars listen, in merry ranks.
With glow-in-the-dark donuts, our feast,
We laugh like crazy, to say the least.

Your snore's a symphony, so divine,
It dances softly, a lullaby line.
While dreaming deeply of cheese and toast,
You wake up to say, 'I love you most!'

Like a raccoon with a shiny prize,
Chasing the glow, see the laughter rise.
In shadows, we scheme, our plans out loud,
Two silly souls, forever proud.

Side by side, under night's embrace,
We find joy in our playful race.
Through nocturnal rays, we hold on tight,
In this wacky love, everything feels right.

Shades of Love's Brilliance

In clashing colors, we stand apart,
Your polka dots dance with my plaid heart.
With every hue, we spark and clash,
Painting our days with a vibrant splash.

You trip while trying to jump the line,
But your laughter's the greatest sign.
In a world where the colors blend,
Our love shines bright, it has no end.

Like ice cream melting in summer sun,
We drip and drop, but we still have fun.
Through silly shades, a love so grand,
We create a masterpiece, hand in hand.

In the palette of life, we find our way,
Mixing colors for every day.
With each new shade, we laugh and tease,
In this vibrant love, we find our ease.

Illuminated Journeys

We hopped on clouds, spun tales so bright,
With weathervanes pointing towards our flight.
In roller skates and hats so tall,
Our laughter echoes, we won't fall.

From silly roads and zig-zag trails,
We ride on dolphins and tell tall tales.
Your hat flies off, a sight to see,
But together, we make history.

Through illuminated skies, we race,
Chasing sunbeams in a wild embrace.
With every twist, and every turn,
Our hearts ignite, together we burn.

So hold my hand, let's take a chance,
In this funny life, let's break the dance.
Through journeys bright, our spirits sing,
In this joyful ride, love's the real thing.

Radiance in Our Silences

In the hush, a chuckle lies,
Like a cat who plots to surprise.
We share winks, sly little grins,
In quiet giggles, our laughter begins.

Whispers dance, tickles in the air,
Mismatched socks with flair, oh, beware!
Our secrets, like glitter, explode,
In silent joy, we're on the same road.

Luminous Echoes of Affection

Your snorts blend with the stars' glow,
As we feign grace in a comedic show.
The universe rolls its eyes at our plight,
Yet together, we shine, a humorous light.

Every eye roll a story to tell,
Like chasing the ice cream truck, oh how swell!
In each playful nudge, a spark ignites,
Creating a glow that makes wrongs feel right.

A Glimmer in the Distance

There's a twinkle like fireflies' dance,
In awkward moments of our goofy stance.
With food on our faces, we burst into glee,
Like parents forced to dance at a three-year spree.

A wink and a grin across the table,
As you pretend to eat my last fable.
Your laughter, a beacon, pulling me near,
In the distance, our chuckles are clear.

Between Shadows

In the shadows, we trip and collide,
With snack raids and secrets we try to hide.
A playful shove, a feathered threat,
But love shines bright, you bet I won't fret.

Our quirks like constellations align,
Dancing through weirdness, a hilarious sign.
In foibles and laughter, we find our groove,
In the mess of our moments, we deeply move.

Stars Alight

Life's a comedy, a script we can make,
With punchlines and pratfalls, a giggly quake.
Underneath stars, we trip on our laughs,
In this wild dance, nobody has gaffs.

Your jokes like rockets, they soar through the night,
Exploding in joy, just pure delight.
With each star-glow, we shimmer and shine,
In our cosmic jest, forever entwined.

Illuminated Paths

In the garden of socks, I found a shoe,
A pair playing hide-and-seek, who knew?
They giggled and swirled, oh what a sight,
Dancing on moonbeams, delightfully bright.

The cat wore a hat, like a royal decree,
He strutted with flair, oh, what a spree!
Chasing shadows that jumped and spun,
Who knew a meow could be so much fun?

Candles in jars, they tell silly tales,
Of pickles in space and fruit that sails.
With laughter erupting like popcorn's cheer,
Even the broccoli joined, oh dear!

So let's walk these paths, where giggles abound,
In the land of the wacky, joy's always found.
Bright moments linger, like glittering swirls,
Join me in laughter, oh silly world!

Whispered Lumens

A cupcake whispered secrets to a pie,
Of sprinkles and cream, oh my, oh my!
They plotted a party with frosting galore,
Inviting the doughnuts, what a fun score!

Bubblegum candles danced on the floor,
Swaying and twirling, oh what a roar!
Jellybeans jumping to a candy beat,
In a sugary riot, life tastes so sweet!

The moon draped a smile on the grinning sun,
As they played tag, saying, 'Let's have some fun!'
Stars winked above with a mischievous gleam,
In the night's rapture, everything's a dream.

So let's giggle with glee, under the light,
With pastries and laughter, our spirits take flight.
Together we shine, a whimsical crew,
Chasing the smiles, just me and you!

Bridges of Illumination

A toaster popped bread with a gleamy cheer,
Said, 'Join me for breakfast, my dear, oh dear!'
The coffee brewed laughter, oh what a sound,
In this morning circus, joy knows no bounds.

The chair did a jig, while the table played flute,
Forks joined the chorus, in a clunky pursuit.
Boiling water hummed a soft serenade,
While kitchen gadgets giggled at the grand parade.

Window blinds swayed to the rhythm of breeze,
Tickling the curtains with giggly tease.
Sunbeams joining in the dance of delight,
Pillow fights under the sheets, oh what a sight!

So let's cross these bridges, where silliness reigns,
With laughter and love, happiness gains.
Skip, hop, and jump through the fun, our goal,
In this bright universe, we shine as a whole!

Pulse of the Daylight

The alarm clock rang, with a croaky tone,
Said, 'Get up, sleepyhead, don't you moan!'
In slippers and pjs, I jumped out of bed,
Tripping on a cat who was under my head.

Ovens were singing, bread rising with glee,
Sausages danced like they're in a spree.
Pancakes flipped high, like dreams in the air,
With syrupy chuckles, no worries, no care.

Sunshine walked in, wearing shades of gold,
Whispered sweet nonsense, daring and bold.
The shadows joined in, with pirouettes grand,
While dust motes leapt up, like grains of sand.

So laugh through the daylight, in joy let's partake,
For every silly moment, is a smile we make.
With a pulse of the sun, let's bounce through the day,
Finding fun in the mundane, in our own quirky way!

The Symphony of Our Shadows

When shadows dance and skip about,
They've got a tune, there's no doubt.
A waltz with laughter in the air,
While funny faces give a scare.

With every giggle and each twist,
We find the notes that can't be missed.
In this odd concert, we unite,
Our shadows sing in pure delight.

From silly moves to jumpy springs,
We orchestrate the silliest things.
A symphony of giggles reigns,
Where joy and laughter break the chains.

So let us frolic, chase the night,
In every shadow, find the light.
Let's play this song, you and me,
And make our shadows dance with glee.

Threads of Light and Life

In threads of laughter, we all weave,
A tapestry no one would believe.
Each silly moment, brightly sewn,
In this great quilt, we've brightly grown.

A string of puns and funny jests,
Together we might pass some tests.
Like clowns who trip but never fall,
We stitch together through it all.

With spools of joy, we bind our hearts,
Creating chaos, artsy parts.
For in this fabric, see us shine,
Threaded through with love divine.

So grab a thread, let's make it right,
We'll knit our dreams in pure delight.
In every loop, a memory drawn,
In threads of life, we carry on.

A Canvas Painted with Understanding

With brushes dipped in joy and fun,
We paint our world beneath the sun.
A canvas filled with every hue,
In strokes of laughter, me and you.

We splash some giggles, toss in glee,
Mix stripes of chaos, paint with free.
In this wild art of life we share,
It's wonderfully odd, yet rare.

Each color tells a funny tale,
With splatters that may sometimes fail.
Yet in the mess, a bond we see,
In every brush, you're close to me.

Let's frame our smiles, hang them high,
Beneath this canvas, we will fly.
Together painting life's display,
With joy and laughter leading the way.

Gleams in the Night

In the night's embrace, we find our spark,
   With goofy grins, we light the dark.
  Each twinkle shines, a joke unfolds,
    In every gleam, a laughter bold.

The moon chuckles at our delight,
As we play games under starlight.
With fireflies joining in our dance,
They join the fun, a glowing chance.

A giggle here, a snicker there,
Even the owls join in the flair.
With every gleam, let's make it bright,
As we share stories until the light.

So here's to nights of joyous cheer,
Where laughter whispers, loud and clear.
In every gleam, a wink, a smile,
Joining our hearts across each mile.

A Spectrum of Shared Moments

In a world of socks and mismatched shoes,
We dance to rhythms, unwritten blues.
With laughter echoing in the halls,
We trip on joy and rise from falls.

A mustard stain on a bright-white shirt,
We giggle at coffee spills and dessert.
With every mishap, we cheer and jest,
In this goofy life, we feel the best.

Our inside jokes float like bubbles in air,
Tickling pink, absurdity everywhere.
From puns that land and fumbles that soar,
We sprinkle fun, with love at the core.

So here's to us, a wacky parade,
In the carnival of life, we've got it made.
With each shared moment, we color the day,
In a spectrum of joy, forever we'll play.

Sparks in the Twilight

In twilight's glow, we roam like sprites,
Chasing fireflies on summer nights.
With silly poses and laughter unbound,
We light the sky without a sound.

A dance-off on the sidewalk tiles,
We flaunt our moves, flash goofy smiles.
With every spark, we touch the stars,
In our universe, no one cares who spars.

Each moment's like a whimsical game,
Where routines clash and humor's to blame.
From awkward jokes to pratfalls grand,
We find connection in the unplanned.

So let's twirl in the dusky embrace,
With laughter as our guiding trace.
As sparks fly up to the evening's dome,
Together we shine, forever at home.

Unity's Warm Embrace

When we gather, it's a comedy show,
With punchlines delivered in swift-flow.
In the heart of chaos, we find our beat,
Sharing silly snacks and dancing on feet.

A pie in the face, who made that mess?
Laughter erupts; it's all part of the excess.
We bond in the silliness, awkward yet bright,
Creating memories that feel just right.

From sloshing drinks to fallen hats,
We cherish the moments, all of the spats.
In every mishap, a treasure we find,
A unity growing, heartstrings entwined.

With giggles that echo through rooms filled with cheer,
We toast to each other, our joys crystal clear.
In the warmth of our friendship, we chase away gloom,
In unity's embrace, there's always more room.

The Light That Knows No Distance

In the distance, our laughter rings true,
Like bright little stars, we sparkle anew.
Though miles may stretch, our spirits collide,
In this odd little world, we're side by side.

With memes that travel through screens through the night,

We share our quirks with pure delight.
From goofy chats to challenges dare,
Distance can't dim the love that we share.

As spoons get bent and stories are spun,
Every shared chuckle is joyously fun.
We may wander far, but here's the twist,
Each laugh we send is a hug not missed.

So here's to the times and the jests we weave,
In every shared moment, we both believe.
Though miles apart, our hearts still dance,
In this wonderful glow, we take a chance.

The Light That Bridges Hearts

In the kitchen, you dance like a chef,
With spaghetti as your partner, oh what a mess!
Your laughter bounces off the walls,
Who knew noodles could be so expressive?

At the park, we chase shadows that play,
Our frisbee's a comet, soaring away.
You giggle like a child on a swing,
As we pretend to be birds—what a day!

We tell secrets to the stars at night,
Joking, they twinkle in pure delight.
Your puns can light up the darkest skies,
Like a firefly circus, oh what a sight!

In moments of silence, our smiles collide,
With silly faces, our hearts open wide.
With every chuckle, we break down the dark,
As the universe joins our joyful ride.

Whispered Luminescence

You wore a cape made of pizza slices,
The superhero of cheesy devices!
When you tell a joke, the moonlight falls,
Echoing laughter that never suffices.

In the garden, we dance with the bees,
While you charm the daisies with jokes, if you please.
I swear the sun chuckles overhead,
As you prance 'round like you're on a breeze!

The tickle of shadows runs down your cheek,
Like the glow of our moments, bright and unique.
We whisper to fireflies, plotting a show,
In the glow of our friendship, there's nothing antique!

With costumes of laughter, we're never alone,
In our world of giggles, we've overgrown.
The stars have their gossip, all about us,
A cosmic comedy we've brightly outshone.

Hidden Colors of Harmony

You mix your emotions like colors of paint,
And with each new hue, you're both sinner and saint.
When you trip over rainbows, it's pure art,
Leaving laughter to blossom, no need for restraint!

As we paint with thoughts in a messy array,
Your wisecracks turn gray skies into play.
Like kids in a candy store, we feast,
On sweet silly jokes that brighten the day!

Even shadows can dance when you're nearby,
Chasing the giggles that sparkle and fly.
In a world of dull moments, you're the burst,
An explosion of crazy—oh how we defy!

In silence, a chuckle can ripple the scene,
With vibes so contagious, it's pure magazine.
Who would've thought our hearts could race,
With hidden colors—a humorous routine!

Shimmering Veils of Understanding

You wear your confusion like a trendy hat,
Saying things like, 'What's a cat in a spat?'
While you ponder the mysteries of why,
It's hard to keep calm with so much chitchat!

In the realm of giggles, we trip and we dive,
Our friendship a comedy, so alive.
You shoot witty comments like sparkles of fun,
With each playful quip, our spirits revive!

When we gaze at stars and slightly lose track,
You say they're just holes to let silliness crack.
In your curious gaze, the cosmos shines bright,
As laughter's the language we don't need to back!

With shimmering veils, we dodge serious talks,
Making pigeons our audience, while laughing and squawk.
Who knew that our silliness could light the way,
Binding us tight like a pair of bright socks?

Illuminating Silences

In the quiet, laughter blooms,
Tickles echo in spare rooms.
Whispers turn to giggles bright,
In shadows, joy ignites the night.

Puns are sprawled on every wall,
Like sticky notes, they never fall.
Banter floats like a friendly kite,
Soaring high, a comical sight.

Muffin crumbs on our retreat,
Chasing crumbs with nimble feet.
We find joy in silly things,
And wear friendship like borrowed rings.

In this space, sounds are a treat,
Where laughter and silence meet.
With every glance, a joke unfolds,
In the brightness, warmth beholds.

Woven from Starlight

Stars giggle in cosmic play,
As we dance in a fateful sway.
Moonlight wraps us in a hug,
While we share a donut mug.

Cotton candy skies collide,
With rainbow dreams we cannot hide.
Each twinkle is a teasing wink,
In this galactic we're on the brink.

We toss wishes like they're confetti,
In mischief, we're always ready.
With laughter echoing through the night,
Our joy takes flight, oh what a sight!

Woven tales of starlit fun,
As we laugh till the morn is done.
In every chat, a giggle grows,
In this world, anything goes.

Kisses of Twilight

As daylight waves its goodbyes,
Silly whispers fill the skies.
Twilight teases with soft sighs,
Like puppies dreaming of pizza pies.

The sun dips low, a quick hide-and-seek,
And shadows play, so sly and cheeky.
Mismatched socks, we're an odd pair,
Laughing loudly without a care.

With every glimmer, mischief starts,
Ticklish moments melt our hearts.
Kisses of dusk, not quite a fight,
Just playful nudges in fading light.

So let's embrace this twilight tease,
With twinkling eyes and wobbly knees.
Each moment melts and sways like this,
Filled with laughter and a moonlit kiss.

Dances in the Sun

Under the sun, we romp and play,
Chasing shadows throughout the day.
Each tumble's met with sprightly cheer,
As laughter rings for all to hear.

Silly hats and shoes askew,
Jumping puddles, just us two.
With every step, a giggle springs,
While the sun dances, oh how it sings.

Umbrellas turned from rain to shade,
In this circus of dreams we've made.
With sun-kissed skin and joyful squeals,
Life's a game, and fun is real.

So grab my hand and twirl with glee,
In this sunlit, carefree spree.
We'll waltz through laughter, spin through light,
In every heartbeat, pure delight.

Aurora of Togetherness

In the kitchen, we dance and prance,
With spatulas and silly chance.
Your socks are striped, oh what a sight,
We cook up joy, with all our might.

Laughter bubbles in the air,
Like soda pop, it fills the square.
Your jokes are cheesy, that's no lie,
But oh, the giggles reach the sky!

We stumble on our feet, so bold,
Like clumsy penguins in the cold.
With every trip and every fall,
We've made a masterpiece, that's all!

So here we stand, side by side,
With love and laughter as our guide.
Let's paint the world in hues so bright,
Together, we'll shine through the night!

Shimmering Moments

Like fireflies in a summer haze,
We flicker bright in funny ways.
You tossed a pillow, I ducked in fright,
Yet somehow, it turned into a flight!

Our plans are swirling like a dance,
In silly hats, we take a chance.
Your puns are worse than a dad's bad song,
But they pull us close where we belong.

We chase the sunset, or maybe not,
A game of tag, with an air-ship shot.
Our laughter echoes through the trees,
Shimmering memories, carried by the breeze.

With every giggle, with every grin,
In this wild ride, we both win.
So hold my hand, let's make a scene,
In shimmering moments, we live the dream!

Sunlit Encounters

The sun decides to play a game,
And in its glow, we stake our claim.
With goofy faces, we take a pose,
A snapshot of the joy that grows.

At picnics, you bring broccoli stew,
I bring the smiles, that much is true.
With ants as guests, we feast and cheer,
In every bite, we hold our dear.

We race the clouds, up to the sky,
You trip in laughter, oh my, oh my!
With every tumble, we softly gleam,
In this wild joke, we share a dream.

So here's to you, my sunny friend,
In goofy ways, our hearts will mend.
With fun as our compass, we'll wander far,
In sunlit encounters, you are my star!

Dappled Affection

Under trees where shadows play,
We find the fun in every day.
You tickle my ribs, I laugh out loud,
Creating ripples in the crowd.

Like dandelions spun in flight,
Your laughter twinkles in the light.
With every joke, we weave a tale,
A tapestry where we both prevail.

The world's a stage, we play our part,
With silly props and all my heart.
We swap our shoes, we giggle loud,
In dappled fields, we feel so proud.

So grab my hand, let's twirl and spin,
In this wild world, let laughter win.
Side by side, let the joy expand,
In the dance of life, an endless band!

Dreamscapes of Togetherness

In a land where socks all match,
Cats wear hats, and dogs just catch.
We sip tea made of gummy bears,
Sharing tales of silly stares.

As we bounce on marshmallow clouds,
Laughing loud with giggling crowds.
Monkeys dance on rainbows bright,
Chasing dreams in pure delight.

With jellybeans for comfy beds,
Eagles dive for flying spreads.
We paint the sky with silly hues,
While wearing mismatched shoes.

In this place where joy is king,
Every bell is made to sing.
Together in our wild embrace,
We giggle at the silliest face.

Warm Glow of Empathy

When your socks are on the wrong feet,
And your breakfast tastes like beet,
I'll be there, your trusty guide,
With laughter as our vibrant tide.

In a world where waffles dance,
And every slip is just a chance,
To find the joy in little things,
Like when a rubber chicken sings.

When life's turns leave you perplexed,
And every plan seems to be hexed,
We'll play hopscotch on a whim,
And make the world a goofy hymn.

A sunny glare on both our backs,
While racing through the grassy tracks,
Together, sharing all the fun,
As we watch the ducks all run.

Shining Through the Silence

In the quiet moments we both share,
I'll slip on socks that don't quite pair.
With my t-shirt worn inside out,
We'll build a fort, there is no doubt!

With whispers soft, we laugh out loud,
Like sneaky squirrels in a crowd.
Tiptoeing on jellybean paths,
Creating giggles and silly laughs.

When the stars are made of candy treats,
And we dance with rhythm in our seats.
We'll twirl and spin in pure delight,
As the moon plays peek-a-boo all night.

In the breaks between each chuckle,
We'll build a castle made of muckle.
In the silence, our hearts still sing,
As we wear laughter like a king.

Pathways Illuminated by Hearts

On a path of gummy worms we tread,
With sunflower hats upon our heads.
We strut like penguins in a race,
With goofy grins upon our face.

Every step, a rhythm found,
As we dance upon the ground.
Bubbles float and tickle our nose,
As we wear mismatched shoes, who knows?

Like honey bees in silly flight,
Zipping past with pure delight.
Our laughter sparks like fireflies,
Lighting up the darkest skies.

With ice cream cones that never drop,
And bubble wrap that never pops,
We stroll beneath the twinkling stars,
As friendship glows, no need for scars.

The Ethereal Realm of Togetherness

In a land of socks, mismatched and bright,
We dance past the fridge, mid-sandwich delight.
Laughter erupts, like gravy from cans,
Our friendship's a buffet, with quirky demands.

Balloons knock the ceiling, they float with a grin,
We reminisce tales where no one can win.
With puns like confetti, we let the jokes fly,
A circus of giggles, oh my, oh my!

Hats piled up high, topped with sprightly glee,
A fashion parade, just two of us free.
We strut in our slippers, they squeak as we roam,
In this wacky dimension, we've both found a home.

So here's to the magic that keeps us in sync,
Like two peas in a pod, or odd shades of pink.
In this realm so absurd, where laughter's the guide,
We'll twirl in our mischief, with joy as our pride.

Fragments of Radiant Unity

We share a shortcake, with cream piled high,
A battle ensues, who gets the last pie?
With forks as our swords, we dive into bliss,
In crumbs of our laughter, we find our true bliss.

Tea spills are common, a splash here and there,
As we swap silly stories of plungers and hair.
With snorts and loud giggles, the neighbors all stare,
We waltz in absurdity, an unplanned affair.

A duet of chaos, we sing out of tune,
Like cats on a rooftop, beneath the full moon.
While socks pair in haste, or pair not at all,
In fragments of unity, we have a grand ball.

So raise a toast now, with juice in a mug,
To moments of mirth, and a warm fuzzy hug.
In our world of hijinks, we're kings of the jest,
Together, my friend, we create the best fest.

Luminescence of Forgotten Moments

Under starlit skies, we chase after dreams,
With roars of pure laughter, rippling like streams.
In old photo albums, the memories play,
We giggle at hairdos from back in the day.

Socks fly through the air, a playful balloon,
As we dance like the fools, to an unsung cartoon.
With mustaches of foam, we raise our disguise,
In moments forgotten, our joy never dies.

Funny hats brought to life, they wobble and sway,
As we plot silly schemes for tomorrow's play.
Our whispers in shadows bring smiles so wide,
With luminescence blooming, we'll take it in stride.

Tickling echoes, while our munchies persist,
In this chaotic moment, how could we resist?
Here's to the laughter, the joy that it sends,
In realms of blunders, we'll always be friends.

Kindred Spirits in Light

A basket of wishes, all fruity and sweet,
We toss in some giggles, and dance on our feet.
With quirky confessions, our hearts intertwine,
In friendship's bright glow, our spirits align.

Bizarre little antics, from morning to dusk,
Like finding lost treasures, or petting a husk.
We laugh till we wheeze, with joy and delight,
In this grand adventure, our souls take to flight.

Juggling our sorrows, like clowns at a show,
Our glee radiates like the sun's warming glow.
Through silly distractions, we take on the night,
As kindred in madness, our bond feels just right.

So here's to our tales, so lively and spry,
To tickles and cackles, beneath the sky high.
In the light of our laughter, we find what is true,
Two odd little peas, forever just "us two."

Lightwoven Bonds

In a world where giggles reign,
We share our laughs like drops of rain.
A wink, a joke, a playful tease,
Finding joy with utmost ease.

Our secrets flicker, shine so bright,
Like fireflies dancing in the night.
With every pun and silly face,
We weave our bonds in a funny embrace.

When life gets tough, we crack a grin,
With laughter's lift, we always win.
A tangle here, a snort or two,
In this bright web, it's me and you.

Together in this light we play,
With goofy thoughts that lead the way.
In our own world of jests and cheer,
The love between us is crystal clear.

Chasing the Dawn

We race the sun with our silly shoes,
Chasing light, we cannot lose.
With coffee spills and sleepy yawns,
We greet the day with silly puns.

The morning sky, a canvas bright,
We paint it with our laughter's light.
Skipping breakfast, we take a chance,
And dance around, a goofy prance.

As shadows fade, our jokes take flight,
We make each moment feel just right.
With each new dawn, we find our groove,
In this mad chase, we always move.

So here we are, heartbeats in tune,
Chasing dawn, singing a happy tune.
In laughter's spark, our spirits soar,
Together shining forevermore.

Embracing the Glow

In a world where humor glows,
We twirl and laugh, and anything goes.
With each misstep, we find delight,
As we embrace the silly sight.

Under the stars, our jokes collide,
Like shooting comets, side by side.
We moonwalk dreams with goofy flair,
In this bright glow, we haven't a care.

With cheesy jokes and funny tales,
We navigate life's winding trails.
A wink, a smile, with every show,
In this bright light, our spirits grow.

So let the world create a fuss,
In our own bubble, there's just us.
Together weaving joy's sweet thread,
In laughter's glow, we're always fed.

Reflections in the Light

In mirrors bright, our joy reflects,
With grins so wide, who'd expect?
A giddy dance, a twirl or spin,
In this bright mirth, we always win.

We leap through puddles, splash and play,
Chasing worries far away.
The sunlight plays upon our face,
In laughter's arms, we find our place.

With every chuckle, brighter we gleam,
Together sharing the silliest dream.
In reflections bright, our spirits align,
Two hearts entwined, in love's design.

So let the world watch this light affair,
In our funny, loving glare.
Together we rise, together we shine,
In this joyful dance, forever divine.

.

Twilight's Embrace

In the dusk, we both trip and fall,
Laughing loudly, we'll rise after all.
Stars above giggle, they know our game,
We stumble and fumble, yet never the same.

Shadows play tricks, they wrap us in cheer,
We dance with the moon, who's had too much beer.
With every turn, our feet spout delight,
In this ruckus, we're twinkling so bright.

Night whispers jokes, the owls hoot along,
We share silly stories, they don't take long.
A comet goes by, it trips on a star,
In this cosmic comedy, we've come so far.

Together we're goofy, no reason to stress,
In twilight's embrace, let's wear our weirdness!
With laughter our lantern, we light up the night,
While the universe chuckles, oh what a sight!

Illuminations of Shared Solitude

When quiet descends, can you hear the sound?
Two hearts giggle when there's no one around.
A light flickers on, but it's just a stray cat,
We both laugh out loud, what's funny in that?

In solitude's cloak, we find hidden jokes,
The walls whisper secrets, like mischievous folks.
A chair squeaks loudly, we both jump in fright,
Yet how we connect in this silence feels right.

We ponder the fridge, what's left for a feast?
That half-eaten taco? It's perfect, at least!
With leftover dreams and a sprinkle of cheese,
Our lonely banquet will bring us some ease.

In shadows of solace, we giggle and glow,
Who needs a crowd when it's you and me, bro?
With laughter our compass, we wander through light,
In shared solitude, the world feels just right!

The Dance of Hidden Glow

Underneath the covers, we giggle so free,
Like robins in spring, we chirp with glee.
The dance of the socks, a mismatched delight,
Our feet do the cha-cha in the glow of the night.

In the corners we hide, we plot and we scheme,
To make even shadows burst out with a beam.
Sparkle confetti, oh where did it go?
Caught in the moment, we bask in the show.

Disguised in plain sight, our laughter takes flight,
The clock on the wall complains, "Not tonight!"
Yet time is forgotten when fun's overhead,
We dance with the silence; it's joy instead.

So here's to the giggles, the jests, and the plays,
In our hidden glow, we frolic through days.
With odd little moves, our hearts do respond,
In this silly waltz, of life's great beyond!

Flashes of Inner Light

Out of the blue, you crack such a grin,
Bright as the sunshine, it draws me right in.
With witticisms flying, they light up the room,
In the spark of the moment, all worries consume.

Like fireflies dancing in twilight's embrace,
Our laughter erupts, it quickens the pace.
Each giggle we share, a flash of delight,
Reminds us that joy is a beautiful sight.

You trip over air, it's a comical plight,
But up you bounce back, an expert in flight.
With every small blunder, we're quick to revive,
In flashes of fun, oh, how we survive!

So let's keep on shining, through blunders and quirks,
In each silly moment, our friendship works.
With humor as fuel, we'll light up the night,
In this game of together, we'll always unite!

Soft Gleams of Kindred Souls

In the kitchen, we cook with flair,
Your socks are mismatched, but who would care?
We laugh at the cat, who's plotting schemes,
While chasing after all our wild dreams.

You steal the fries from my lunch plate,
Declaring it's love, sealed with fate.
With every wink and silly dance,
We light up the world with our goofy chance.

When we play cards, the laughs just flow,
You yell 'Cheat!' as I win the show.
Yet in the end, it's all just fun,
For in our hearts, we've already won.

So here's to us and our funny spree,
A duo, together, as bright as can be.
In every giggle and every cheer,
Together forever, we've nothing to fear.

Flickers of Unity

Two peas in a pod, or so they say,
Yet one of us snores the night away.
With your dreadful jokes and my crazy puns,
We dance in the kitchen, oh, how fun!

In the park, we race, but I fall flat,
You burst out laughing as I lie like a mat.
With silly faces and playful shoves,
We prove that friendship is what we love.

You claim your dog is a Hollywood star,
While mine thinks he's the best by far.
We stroll through life, hand in hand,
With laughter and giggles, together we stand.

Though some may see us as quite absurd,
In our universe, our spirits are stirred.
Forever united, we'll sing out loud,
Creating a symphony, goofy and proud.

Celestial Bonds of Light

We stargaze while eating a midnight snack,
You spill the popcorn, as usual, whack!
With constellations swirling in our eyes,
We ponder if aliens wear funny ties.

You challenge me to a moonlit race,
Tripping over shadows, we're in a chase.
Laughter echoes in the cool night air,
A symphony crafted with joy and flair.

With bright ideas that spark like stars,
You say life's better when it's full of jars.
We collect our memories in funny notes,
Sailing through life, in our laughter, we float.

Under the glow of a million lights,
We find our joy in the silliest sights.
For in this universe, chaotic yet grand,
We shine like galaxies, hand in hand.

In Every Pulse, a Flicker

In the morning, we dance with glee,
While stumbling over the cat's next spree.
With a wink and a nudge, we embrace the day,
Chasing our cares and worries away.

You declare that breakfast is a sport,
As you scramble eggs and somehow contort.
With laughter erupting like bubbles of fun,
We toast to the chaos, for we're never done.

Every heartbeat sings a vivid tune,
As we pull off pranks under the moon.
With jokes that sparkle in our shared glow,
Together, we flourish, together we grow.

In every pulse, our spirits ignite,
Creating a chorus that shines oh so bright.
With friendship that blossoms in the silliest ways,
We treasure each flicker, all of our days.

Vows in Radiance

In the glow of our laughter, we pledge to be bright,
With jokes that keep us glowing, from morning till night.
Your puns light up the room, like a holiday flare,
In this comedy club, we're the best little pair.

Wearing socks that don't match, that's the style we choose,
A bold fashion statement, we both can't excuse.
With a wink and a grin, we stumble on love,
As we dance through the chaos, like stars up above.

You trip on your shoelace, I giggle and dive,
Together we tumble, in this demented jive.
Side by side we conquer, the world's a big stage,
With each goofy moment, we turn another page.

So here's to the blunders, and all that we share,
In this whirlwind of joy, we float through the air.
With vows of pure laughter, our hearts cozy tight,
The funniest journey—what a marvelous sight!

The Light We Share

As we sit side by side with snacks piled high,
Your cheesy remarks are the cherry on pie.
We scribble our dreams on napkins and trays,
In this kingdom of snacks, we rule all our days.

Your puns have a sparkle, like fireflies at dusk,
As we dodge the dull moments—never a husk.
With a wink and a nod, we keep the fun near,
In this circus of life, you're the clown I hold dear.

Whispers and giggles, in our secret hideout,
With laughter echoing, casting shadows about.
Mismatched socks lead the way to our art,
In this game called romance, you've mastered the smarts.

So let our days twinkle, like stars they will light,
With every quirk and jest, we brighten the night.
In this endless fun ride, we'll conquer the fare,
For in every chuckle, I find love's sweet flare!

Shadows Transformed

In the shadows we dance, with a tiptoe and twirl,
You crack a bad pun, and I give it a whirl.
With each silly moment, our worries take flight,
As we turn shadows bright, like lanterns at night.

Your goofball expressions can lighten the dark,
And when my heart sinks, you're the boat, I'm the ark.
Through tickles and giggles, we'll shift every mood,
With a sprinkle of laughter, our fears are subdued.

We wear capes of folly, in this carnival show,
Scaling the heights of delight like a wild rodeo.
As shadows transform, we embrace folly's song,
In the dance of our lives, where no one's wrong.

So here's to the nights when we let out a roar,
With humor our lantern, we'll light up the floor.
In this journey together, let silliness reign,
For love in its essence is humor unchained!

Kindled Journeys

On this path of mischief, our laughter ignites,
With jokes lighting candles on even the nights.
Hand in hand we wander, like kids on the run,
In a world full of fumbles, we've already won.

You joke that I'm lost, but I feel quite at home,
In this whimsical world, together we roam.
With whimsy as our compass, we chart out the fun,
Twirling through life, till the day is all done.

Through each silly stumble, your smile shines bright,
As we skip through the meadows, full of sheer delight.
Here's to our travels, where whimsy's the guide,
In this kooky adventure, you're my joyful ride.

So let's keep on laughing, while the stars keep aglow,
With hearts full of giggles, we're never too slow.
Our kindled journeys, in laughter's embrace,
Are the beats of our hearts, in this timeless race!

A Dance of Shadows and Light

In a world of giggles and cheer,
Where shadows dance without a fear,
A waltz of whimsy spins the night,
Tickling stars till they burst with light.

Silly hats tipped just askew,
Once somber clouds now blush in hue,
We chase the moon, just for a laugh,
On bumpy roads, we share our path.

Laughter carries on the breeze,
While shadows play, they aim to tease,
With every twirl, the darkness fades,
As giggles light the happy glades.

We trip on giggles, fall on grace,
In this quirky, funny place,
With every step, a joke takes flight,
In our dance of shadows and light.

Circles of Warmth

In the circle of friends, we whoop,
Giggling like an uproarious troop,
Warmed by laughter, sun-bright and clear,
Each joke a hug, each laugh a cheer.

Fluffy pillows and snacks galore,
Footsie fights on the living room floor,
We swap our tales, the wild and weird,
In our cozy nest, no spirits get seared.

A sprinkle of antics, a dash of glee,
Turn up the fun, and let it be free,
Circle dance 'round the kitchen stove,
We mimic chefs, in laughter we rove.

As shadows cling and friendships grow,
A warm embrace melts the evening glow,
Each chuckle a spark that warms our night,
In circles of warmth, everything's right.

The Fireflies of Connection

In fields of giggles, we ignite,
Little fireflies dancing in the night,
Their glow is silly, their flight is wise,
Chasing each other 'neath the starlit skies.

One zap and zoom, a flicker, a fizz,
Their bright little bodies bask in the whizz,
We join their party, laughter in tow,
Creating sparks, sharing the glow.

When dusk draws nigh and giggles ring clear,
Fireflies share secrets that only we hear,
With a wink and a flicker, they start to play,
Our hearts in bloom, lighting the way.

So let's gather round in this whimsical light,
For connections that glimmer make spirits so bright,
With each laugh we capture, we join in the fun,
Like fireflies of joy, we light up the run.

Echoes of Our Inner Glow

In the caverns of laughter, our echoes ignite,
Bouncing off walls, oh, what a delightful sight,
Silly tunes sung, harmonies clash,
A cacophony bold, a vibrant splash.

Each giggle strains the seams of the night,
Like a party of shadows, oh, what a delight!
We tap dance through time, in our own little show,
With echoes of joy, our spirits will grow.

Can you hear it? The chuckles ring true,
A chorus of quirks, each note overthrew,
Through the rumbles and roars, our hearts all aglow,
Together we twinkle, with every echo.

So let's bask in the fun, let the laughter unfold,
In the echoes we find, a magic to hold,
With voices entwined, we create a tableau,
As echoes of us light the night with a glow.